✚

COPTIC ORTHODOX PATRIARCHATE

I0162803

See of St. Mark

ORDINATION OF WOMEN
&
HOMOSEXUALITY

BY
H.H. POPE SHENOUDA III

COPA

Two Lectures by His Holiness Pope Shenouda III

First Edition Published by:
Coptic Orthodox Publishers Association
50 Netherford Road
London SW4 6AE
Tel: 01-622 0166

H.H. Pope Shenouda III
117th Pope and Patriarch of Alexandria
and the See of St Mark

CONTENTS

Priesthood in the Holy Bible
Priesthood in Church Tradition
Who Is the Head of the Church?
Virgin Mary and Priesthood
Deaconesses and Serving the Altar
Women and Priest's Work
Church Sacraments Delivered to Men
Responsibilities of Women
Questions

INTRODUCTION

The authentic views of the Coptic Orthodox Church on the two controversial subjects of 'The Ordination of Women' and 'Homosexuality' have been clearly and authoritatively expressed by His Holiness Pope Shenouda III in two lectures given on the 26th of November 1990. A great number of clergymen from various churches heard His Holiness give evidence from the Holy Bible and from tradition relating these two subjects, to which the Orthodox Church is gravely opposed..

Fuad H. Megally, PhD.

HOMOSEXUALITY

I am very glad to have the opportunity to speak to the ministers of the Church of England. I mean, to speak to the angels of the Church and the ministers of our Lord; those who were mentioned in the Book of Revelation as stars in the right hand of our Lord.

I thank God that He has given me the opportunity to speak to those to whom the Lord said: *"You shall be witnesses to Me."* *(Acts 1:8).* *'Witnesses to Me'*, that means, witnesses to the truth; to the Holy Bible; to the commandments of God; and to what the Holy Spirit has passed on to the Churches.

I want to speak to you about numerous things, and if you would like a discussion about a particular issue, I am willing to discuss it with you.

The Holiness Of The Church

The first matter is the holiness of the Church. In the holy Creed we say: "We believe in one holy Church". This holy Church is Apostolic and Universal. In the Apostolic age, **all believers were called saints.** A believer in the teachings of the Bible means a saint, because we are sanctified with faith, sanctified in baptism, sanctified in the holy Chrism, and sanctified by the work of the Holy Spirit in our hearts.

We are not merely human beings, we are temples of the Holy Spirit, and the Holy Spirit is abiding in us, as it is written in the First Epistle to the Corinthians, chapters 3 and 6. As temples of the Holy Spirit, we should have communion with the Holy Spirit. The work of a believer is not simply the work of an individual, but rather the work of the Holy Spirit itself in that person, who is a temple of the Holy Spirit.

We are also the image of God, and we project to the world the image of God. The world sees in our conduct and in our behaviour what demonstrates that we are really children of God.

At the beginning of the Epistles of Saint Paul to the Romans, he writes: *"Paul, a servant of Jesus Christ, called to be an Apostle, separated to the gospel of God.. to all who are in Rome, beloved of God, called to be saints"* (Rom. 1: 1,7). Also, in another Epistle, he writes: *"To the church of God which is at Corinth, to those who are sanctified in Christ Jesus, called to be saints"* (1Cor. 1: 2). Further still, in the Second Epistle, he says: *"To the church of God which is at Corinth, with all the saints who are in all Achaia "* (2Cor. 1: 1).

When he writes to Ephesus, he sends his greetings to all the saints in Ephesus, and to the Philippians he does the same. Again, when he writes to the Hebrews, for example, in chapter 3, he writes to those who are called to the Divine Call, who are also saints.

If we are supposed to be saints, then how must we behave, and, more importantly, how can we convey that holy Image to the world?

In the Apostolic age, not everyone was allowed to enter the Church. Only those who were worthy could attend the holy Eucharist and partake in the Blood and Body of our Lord Jesus Christ. This holy life is what we are called to, because we are the children of a holy Father. Saint Peter speaks about this point and says: *"...as obedient children, not conforming yourselves to the former lusts, as in your ignorance; but as He who called you is holy, you also be holy in all your conduct, because it is written, 'Be holy, for I am holy '"* (1Pet. 1: 14-16), and this was written in Leviticus (Lev. 11: 44).

Holy people do not live in the lust of the flesh, but they behave according to the Spirit.

A holy person has two characteristics. The first is that his flesh is guided by the spirit; by his human spirit. And the second is that his spirit, his human spirit, is guided by the Spirit of God. So the Spirit of God is guiding the whole person; guiding both the spirit and the body, and hence that person should be holy in spirit and in body.

Let me read some verses from chapter 8 of the Epistle of Saint Paul to the Romans about the body and the spirit. The holy Apostle says: *"There is therefore now no condemnation to those who are in Christ Jesus, who do not walk according to the flesh, but according to the Spirit"* (Rom. 8: 1). And in verse 5, he says: *"For those who live according to the flesh set their minds on the things of the flesh, but those who live according to the Spirit, the things of the Spirit. For to be carnal minded is death, but to be spiritually minded is life and peace. Because the carnal mind is enmity against God, for it is not subject to the law of God, nor indeed can be"* (Rom. 8: 5-7). And then he says: *"... if Christ is in you, the body is dead because of sin, but the Spirit is life because of righteousness "* (Rom. 8: 10). Then he says: *"Therefore, brethren, we are debtors- not to the flesh, to live according to the flesh. For if you live according to the flesh you will die; but if by the Spirit you put to death the deeds of the body, you will live. For as many as are led by the Spirit of God, these are sons of God"* (Rom. 8:12-14). Here, Saint Paul depicts the sons of God as those who are led by the Spirit of the Lord.

Let me now venture to speak about a subject that is rather contentious, and is currently quite outspread, and that needs the grace of our Lord to be overcome; this subject of homosexuality. I am sorry to even have to speak about this issue, it should not be a matter of discussion.

Homosexuality Is Against Nature

Homosexuality is against nature because sexual relations are permitted only within the confines of marriage, and marriage is only permitted between a man and a woman, male and female. Hence, any sexual conduct outside these confines can only be described as an abnormality; an act against nature.

When our Lord Jesus Christ discussed the issue of Homosexuality with the scribes and Pharisees, as written in the

11

Gospel of Saint Matthew chapter 19 and the Gospel of Saint Mark chapter 10, He said: *"From the beginning.. God 'made them male and female '"*, man and woman. This is the proper way of nature and the will of our Lord form the beginning of creation.

But when people behaved according to the lust of the flesh in the Old Testament, they received severe punishment from God, as at the time of the Flood when only the pure, the eight people in Noah's Ark, were saved, and all others perished. Also the people of Sodom, who were unclean, were burned with fire. They also behaved according to the lust of the flesh, the lust of the body; they were unclean in their spirit.

Homosexuals Shall Not Enter The Kingdom Of Heaven

Carnal people cannot inherit the kingdom of heaven. We read this in the Book of Revelation, chapter 21, where it speaks about the heavenly Jerusalem and says: *"But there shall by no means enter it anything that defiles, or causes an abomination"* (Rev. 21: 27).

Homosexuals Were Punished By Death

We read that homosexuality is a kind of abomination which in the Old Testament was punishable by death. If we, for example, read Leviticus, chapter 18, verse 22, God says: *"You shall not lie with a male as with a woman. It is an abomination."* And also in the Book of Leviticus, chapter 20, verse 13, *"If a man lies with a male as he lies with a woman, both of them have*

12

committed an abomination. They shall surely be put to death. Their blood shall be upon them."

Homosexuality Condemned In The New Testament

Of course, the New Testament is no less pure than the Old Testament. So we find at least four examples against homosexuality. In Romans chapter one, in the First Epistle to the Corinthians chapter 6, in the Epistle of Saint Jude, and in the Epistle to Timothy. I will now read some of these verses to remind us of the teachings of the Holy Bible.

Example (1)

In Romans chapter one, it is written: *"For the wrath of God is revealed from heaven against all ungodliness and unrighteousness of men who suppress the truth in unrighteousness."* How is the wrath of God revealed? Verse 24 says: *"Therefore God also gave them up to uncleanness, in the lusts of their hearts, to dishonour their bodies among themselves."* 'Gave them up', this means that the grace of God has left them, that they were forsaken to their own uncleanness to dishonour their bodies. In such abnormality they debase the flesh.

The honour of the body is to be the temple of the Holy Spirit. But if it is abused then it is a dishonour to the body. *"For this reason God gave them up to vile passions. For even their women exchanged the natural use for what is against nature. Likewise also the men, leaving the natural use of the woman, burned in their lust for one another, men with men committing what is shameful, and receiving in themselves the penalty of their error which was due"* (Rom. 1: 26,27).

In his Epistle to the Romans, Saint Paul also spoke about the debased minds, and about things which are not fitting. So, when he says: *'exchanged the natural use for what is against nature'*, it means that homosexuality is against nature. Furthermore, he says that it is an act of uncleanness, an act that dishonours of the body and that is worthy of punishment. Thus, according to the teachings of Saint Paul, homosexuality is not only an act against nature, as was created by our Lord, it is shameful and abominable.

Example (2)

In the First Epistle to the Corinthians, chapter 6, the Apostle says: *"Do not be deceived. Neither fornicators, nor idolaters, nor adulterers, nor homosexuals, nor sodomites... will inherit the kingdom of God"* (1Cor. 6: 9). None of these will inherit the kingdom of God.

As for living in the Spirit and not according to the flesh, he also says: *"Flee sexual immorality. Every sin that a man does is outside the body, but he who commits sexual immorality sins against his own body"* (1Cor. 6: 18). What is meant by 'his own body'? It means that he is sinning against the temple of the Holy Spirit. The Apostle says: *"... do you not know that your body is the temple of the Holy Spirit who is in you, whom you have from God, and you are not your own?"* (1Cor. 6: 19).

14

Your body is not your own; your body is the temple of the Holy Spirit.

When a person sins against his body, it means that he is separating himself from the Holy Spirit. Light and darkness cannot exist together in one place. From the beginning God separated light from darkness (Gen. 1). Therefore, we cannot have the Holy Spirit abiding in our body if we sin against it by what is shameful.

The Apostle says: *"...glorify God in your body and in your spirit which are God's"* (1Cor. 6: 20), meaning that both the body and the spirit belong to God, and hence should be glorified. Also, in chapter 3 he adds: *"Do you not know that you are the temple of God and that the Spirit of God dwells in you? If anyone defiles the temple of God, God will destroy him. For the temple of God is holy, which temple you are"* (1Cor. 3: 16,17).

In the First Epistle to the Corinthians, chapter 6, the Apostle also says: *"Do you not know that your bodies are members of Christ? Shall I then take the members of Christ and make them members of a harlot? Certainly not!"* (1Cor. 6: 15). We are the members of Christ because we are His body and His bones. Saint Paul says: *"It is no longer I who live, but Christ lives in me"* (Gal. 2: 20). **So, if Christ lives in us, how can we abuse our bodies in such ways, how can we defile the members of Christ, the temple of the Holy Spirit?** How can we abuse and dishonour the holy image of God by living in the lust of the flesh? This is against holy life and against chastity.

Example (3)

In his Epistle, Saint Jude says: *"...as Sodom and Gomorra, and the cities around them in a similar manner to these, having given themselves over to sexual immorality and gone after strange flesh, are set forth as an example, suffering the vengeance of eternal fire"* (Jude 7).

Example (4)

In the First Epistle to Timothy, the Apostle says: *"...knowing this: that the law is not made for a righteous person, but for the lawless and insubordinate, for the ungodly and for sinners, for the unholy and profane, for murderers of fathers and murderers of mothers, for manslayers, for fornicators, for sodomites"* (1Tim. 1: 9,10). Saint Paul includes 'sodomites', or homosexuals, among the murderers, the lawless and the ungodly.

Hence, this sin was condemned in both the Old and the New Testaments. So, can we disobey God in order to please some sinners? Is it not better to show them the right way than to let them lose their sanctity and be punished in eternal life? Or let them depend on the Church making this matter lawful?

Homosexuality Is Against Health

I think that in our present day, our Lord God has given us a grand warning in the form of AIDS. A warning to those who subject their bodies to such defilement. Unfortunately people are no longer fearful, even of such a dreadful disease.

Homosexuality Is Against ManHood

How can a person who is used as a woman be called a man? He is deprived of his manhood and is not considered to be a man any longer.

Homosexuality Is Against the Good Name of Christianity

What may be said of Christianity in its supreme ideology? Christianity teaches the sublime ideas of spirituality. How can other religions have any idea about this spiritual life if they know that there is homosexuality in the Church and that the Church is discussing whether it is wrong or right?

Church life should be a life of holiness. A holy person is a member of the Church, but the unholy is not a member of the Church at all. And this is what was mentioned in the Book of Acts, chapter 2, verse 47, where it is written: *"And the Lord added to the church daily those who were being saved"*. The Lord added to the Church those who were being saved because the Church is a congregation of Saints; an abundance of holiness.

Homosexuality Is Against the Holy Sacraments

What can we say about the renewal of life in Christianity if such defilement exists inside the Church? How can we say that we received the new life? ... the renewal of life? ... the new birth? What kind of new birth have we received if we have such defilement among our members? What can we say about salvation? What kind of salvation is it? About baptism, what kind of baptism is it? What can we say about holy Chrism when we are faced with such defilement?

Homosexuality is against the Sacrament of Marriage, and it is also against self-control. People who suffer homosexuality should be ashamed. If they knew the meaning of spiritual life, they could not confess that they are homosexuals. It is quite inconceivable that anyone can lose their sense of shame and openly confess to being homosexuals. It is even more unbelievable is that such people ask for their human rights as homosexuals.

Rights For Homosexuals

What rights are there for homosexuals? **Their only right is to be led to repentance.** But to live in such defilement of the body, in such dishonour of the body, in such abomination and sin, and then ask for their so called human rights unthinkable! Furthermore, being encouraged and defended by some of the members of the Church, they ask to be ordained priesthood, while still practising homosexuality, this is simply beyond belief!

Homosexual Priests

What may members of the congregation say when they know that their priest is homosexual, and that he holds the Body and Blood of our Lord Jesus Christ?

How can a homosexual priest lead the congregation to holy life without having repented, without having confessed, without changing his life? If he cannot repent how can he guide others to repentance? If he cannot control himself, how can he guide others to such control? If he cannot enjoy the beauty of holy life, how can he speak about holy life? **If he leads a carnal life, how can he guide others to live a spiritual life?**

What will be said about the teachings of Christianity if such abominations take place in the Church itself?

Homosexuality and Love

It is claimed that homosexuality is simply love between man and man. No, my brothers, love should be spiritual and pure. We love others in purity. We love others in the Spirit. And loving others should not be against our love for God, because our Lord Jesus Christ said *'He who loves father, son, wife, sister, or brother, more than Me, is not worthy of me, is not worthy to be My disciple.'* We cannot love any other person more than our Lord Jesus Christ. Every love which we have should be love in the Lord. We love in the Lord, not outside, not against.

It is not love, but lust, and there is a great difference between love and lust. The word 'love' is not suitable for such a relation, because in the Gospel, we say *'God is love.'* How can we say 'Homosexuality is love'? It is not love, it is a physical lust, lust of the flesh, and a lust which should be corrected.

If a man loves another man, can he abuse the man whom he loves? Is this love or destruction? If a man really loves another man, can he lead this man to lose his eternity and be punished in eternal life? Is it love to make another lose his image, the image of God?

Homosexual by Nature

Another excuse given is that such a person is born that way. If he is born that way, we need to heal him, to purge him, to correct him, to pray for him, to guide him to repentance, to cure him medically and spiritually. But not to say to him: "Alright, we accept you as a member of the Church and give you the Body and Blood of our Lord." It cannot be said that a person is homosexual by nature. Surely, it is the result of a traumatic experience in life, and this can be corrected.

We have in the history of the Church many saints who were fornicators before being saints, before repentance, and they were corrected. They were not homosexuals, but they were fornicators; the same sin but not abnormal. Saint Augustine is a good example. Saint Moses the Black is another example. Saint Pelagia is another example, and there are many others, and through the grace of God, through the work of pastoral care, they were corrected. We cannot accept homosexuality, for if we do, it means that we allow such an abomination, it means that we permit that person to remain in sin and not repent. Moreover, it means that homosexuals have rights, one of which is to be ordained as priests.

The Spiritual Way of Pleasing Others

We cannot flatter people at the expense of the commandment of God. May I read you one or two verses from the First Epistle to the Galatians: *"For do I now persuade men, or God? Or do I seek to please men? For if I still pleased men, I would not be a bondservant of Christ"* (Gal. 1: 10). If 1 go on pleasing men in contradiction with the commandment of God, then I will not be the servant of Christ.

If I want to please men in a correct way, then I should guide them to repentance. This is the spiritual way of pleasing others, not to let them stay in sin and perish.

What is the benefit in pleasing other if such pleasure leads to condemnation? In the heavenly kingdom, in the kingdom of God, no person who lives in defilement is allowed to enter. No fornicators, nor sodomites, may enter the kingdom of our Lord, as is clearly expressed in the teachings of Saint Paul, Saint Jude, Saint Peter, and many others?

Once I read a book written by one of the clergymen -I do not want to say, one of the bishops- defending homosexuality. He began to attack Saint Paul and say that he is abnormal. Can we please men to the extent where we speak against Apostles? Against a person that was elected by God Himself in a

21

miraculous apparition, and chosen to be the Apostle for the Gentiles; to be our Apostle, for we were Gentiles. Is it acceptable that we try to please men, even if it means going against the teachings of the Lord?

I now return to the first words I said to you. I said I am happy, I am glad, to be among the persons who are chosen to witness to the Lord. Our Lord said: *"But you shall receive power when the Holy Spirit has come upon you; and you shall be witnesses to Me."* As for homosexuals, He said that without repentance, they will perish. This judgement of our Lord was repeated twice in the chapter of Saint Luke's Gospel, chapter 13, verses 3 and 5. It is written: *"I tell you, no; but unless you repent you will all likewise perish"* (v. 3), and in verse 5: *"I tell you, no; but unless you repent you will all likewise perish."*

So, can we say to such sinners, to whom our Lord said: *"...unless you repent you will all likewise perish"*, 'no, no, no, we will find excuses for you. The Church loves you and wants to search for excuses, so that you may remain in sin and not perish?' It is not within our power, I repeat, it is not within our power to justify sins, or to please sinners. Instead, we should be trying to guide them to repentance.

The Way to Repentance

Initially, a person who sins may be embarrassed, and cannot confess to this abomination. However, if that person openly declares his homosexuality, and begins to seek his rights as a homosexual, without seeking repentance, and even goes so far as to ask to be ordained priesthood, then this is an outrage.

However, if we make it clear to that person that such actions are sinful and against the will of God, then perhaps his conscience may act against him, always condemning him and reproaching him: 'You should repent. You must change your ways'.

The Authority Of Clergymen

In the Gospel of Saint Matthew, chapter 18, our Lord Jesus Christ gave His servants, the Apostles, the priests, authority, saying: *"I say to you whatever you bind on earth will be bound in heaven, and whatever you loose on earth will be loosed in heaven"* (Matt. 18: 18). Whatever you bind or loose should be according to the Bible, in harmony with the teachings of the Bible, in obedience to the commandments of God, but whatever you bind or loose against the Bible will not be accepted. How? If we read the Epistle to the Galatians, chapter 1, verses 8 and 9, we find some very fearful words. It is written: *"But even if we (the Apostles), or an angel from heaven, preach any other Gospel to you than what we have preached to you, let him be accursed'* (Gal 1:8). This is also repeated in verse 9, "If anyone preaches any other gospel to you than what you have received, let him be accursed" (Gal. 1:9).

Our duty as Clergymen is to guide people through the commandments of God. We have no power, nor any authority, to give declare laws against the laws of God. So, why did our Lord give us authority, and how can this authority to bind and loose be explained? Perhaps we can find an explanation in what was written in the prophecy of Malachi, chapter 2, verse 7: *"For the lips of a priest should keep* *knowledge, and people should seek the law from his mouth; for he is the messenger of the Lord of hosts"* (Mal 2:7). People take the law of the Lord from the priest's mouth because, when it comes to God's teachings, he is more knowledgeable than any other member of the congregation. He is the teacher; the guide. So he binds according to the law of God which he knows quite well, and he looses according to the law of God, and never in contradiction, as Saint Paul said: *"If we, or an angel from heaven..."* As Saint Basil of Caesaria Cappadocia said: *"Saint Paul dared to anathematize angels."*

The Grave Responsibility Of The Clergy

What then should we say to people? There is a commandment given by God in the Old Testament. It is repeated twice in the same prophecy of Ezekiel, in chapter 3, and again in chapter 33. May I read you some of the words said by God to Ezekiel: "Son of man, I have made you a watchman (to watch people) for the house of Israel; therefore hear a word from My mouth, and give them warning from Me: When I say to the wicked, *'You shall surely die,'* and you give him no warning, nor speak to warn the wicked from his wicked way, to save his life, **that same wicked man shall die in his iniquity, but his blood will require at your hand"** (Ezek. 3: 17,18).

We are pastors. How can we suffer that the blood of these wicked persons who will perish be required from us? We should warn them and say to them: "This way leads you to destruction". And at the same time God says: *"Yet, if you warn the wicked, and he does not turn from his wickedness, nor from* *his wicked way, he shall die in his iniquity; but you have delivered your soul'* (Ezek. 3: 19).

The same words are also mentioned in chapter 33, because our Lord God wants to emphasise this point. *"So you, son of man: I have made you a watchman for the house of Israel, therefore you shall hear a word from My mouth and warn them for Me. When I say to the wicked, 'O wicked man, you shall surely die!' and you do not speak to warn the wicked from his way, that wicked man shall die in his iniquity,. but his blood I will require at your hand"* (Ezek. 33: 7,8).

We must fear such condemnation. We must warn the wicked and say to them: 'This is the way of death. If you walk according to the flesh you will die; you should obey the commandments of God.' If we love our children in a spiritual way we should guide them to repentance; we should try to purge them, to cleanse them, to heal them, to save them, not to justify their sins. This is not good for them nor for us. They will perish and their blood will be required at our hands.

The following are some of the questions asked by members of the congregation and the answers given by His Holiness:

Question 1

We repeat in the Nicene Creed, I believe in one holy Catholic Apostolic Church". As the Catholic and Apostolic

Church is divided, how can we claim it to be holy? How can holiness and division go together?

Of course this is a tragedy, and for this reason we are trying to work toward Christian unity. We are trying to be one in faith, and one in theology and in doctrine. Our Lord God does not accept this division because in the Gospel of Saint John chapter 10, which we call the chapter of the Good Shepherd, it is clear that He wants the Church to be one flock, for One Shepherd, and this Shepherd is our Lord Jesus Christ. And also in Saint John's Gospel, chapter 17, He asks the Father for His disciples, for the whole Church, to be one, saying: *"...that they may be one just as We are one."* There is no unity more mystical than the unity between the Father and the Son. Of course, separation and division is not a holy matter and for this reason, we are working for the unity of the Church.

Question 2

While we are alive, is it not possible to enjoy bodily pleasures without hurting others, while striving for spiritual ascendancy?

For this reason we said that this bodily pleasure, according to your expression, is enjoyed in marriage and between male and female, but not against nature, not against the commandment of God. As we enjoy bodily pleasures in eating food and delicacies, and control ourselves in the days of fasting, a person may also enjoy bodily pleasures to a certain extent, not to be against his spirit, not to be against the commandment of God, not to be against nature, not to be against purity of heart, and many pleasures are given to us, but not abnormal pleasures.

Question 3

How can we bring healing to people of homosexual tendency who wish to be healed of that tendency and to walk the way of holiness? How may we help them?

The first point on which I spoke was that the Church cannot say that their wrong way is acceptable, this is against the essence of the teachings the Bible. We cannot pass their acts as acceptable behaviour, and excuse them for supposedly being born that way. Sin is sin, whatever the reasons are.

In order to help them, firstly say to them: "This is a sin. This is an abomination", and then let them enjoy the spiritual life. A person who tastes the sweetness of spiritual life may leave such a way of abomination. Because people are always occupied with worldly matters, they do not give time for prayer, for contemplation, for spiritual songs, for reading the Bible, for reading spiritual books, so their spirits become very weak, and such weak spirits cannot resist temptation. If we try to strengthen their spirits, to let them practise spiritual ways, as I said, they get better.

Also, we must pray for them, fast for them, celebrate Holy Masses for them, we must try to help them by using all spiritual means. If there is a situation that requires medical treatment, then let them try it. But, whatever the circumstances, we cannot justify their sins. It is not within our authority as clergymen or pastors.

Question 4

Does the Church see the sexual desire in marriage between husband and wife as lust or good appetite?

Saint Augustine said that it is something attractive from nature to help the act. First marriage was for giving birth to children and to let the world continue, but if there is nothing attractive in such a matter, perhaps people will not have sexual intercourse. As with food, if food is not delicious and of good appetite (I may use appetite here for food), people will not eat and they will die. So God put something attractive in the nature of these matters in order that the act may be completed. But some people who have full love for God may not practise such matters very frequently.

There is something said by Saint Paul in the seventh chapter of the first Epistle to the Corinthians, he said: *"Do not deprive one another except with consent for a time, that you may give yourselves to fasting and prayer, and come together again so that Satan does not tempt you because of your lack of self-control"* (1Cor. 7: 5). And at the beginning he said that when we practise fasting we need self-control to abstain from food. At the same time, if a person, if a husband or wife, can be away from the other partner, in order to practise fasting and prayer in a useful way for the spirit, it should be in consent. The two should approve of the matter, if not, we cannot cause offence for the other partner; this will not be "with consent".

You cannot take everything that your body craves. Solomon, the wisest person, said that he gave himself all kinds of pleasure, and what was the conclusion? I will read what Solomon said: *"Whatever my eyes desired I did not keep from them. I did not withhold my heart from any pleasure"* (Eccl. 2: 10). And what was the end? It was against him and he found that *"all was vanity and grasping for the wind"* (Eccl. 2: 11). A person may take from the pleasures of the world to a certain extent, yet self-control from time to time.

Question 5

How should we relate our Lord's assurance that the wheat and tares will continue together until the end, to the stress on all members of the Church being called to be saints?

Of course, the tares are not members in the Church. The wheat are the elect and the tares are the work of the devil, as our Lord God explained this parable in the thirteenth chapter of Saint Matthew's Gospel, saying that the wheat is the work of God and the tares the work of the devil.

There is sin and there is holy life. Of course, we cannot say that the kingdom of God covers the whole world, but the work of the Church is to have plenty of wheat and to guide the tares to be wheat if possible. This is our duty; to correct others. But of course our Lord Jesus Christ spoke about the tares in this parable as the persons who will perish (not to be corrected). But in the Church we have only wheat.

The Church in its identity is a group of saints worshipping God together. They are holy vessels in which the Holy Spirit works. The definition of the Church is people who are the image of God, who are the true sons of God, who always keep the image of God, have communion with the Holy Spirit, and lead holy lives. These are the true members of the Church; tares are not the true members of the Church.

Question 6

Can we suggest that different branches of one whole may not be evil but that they may all be partakers of God's truth?

Of course we should distinguish between evil and good. There are many kinds of good ways, as for example, marriage and virginity. They are two holy ways which guide to God. But we cannot say that chastity and fornication are two ways which guide to God. Of course not. There may be a kind of variety but inside holiness and not outside holiness, and this is acceptable.

For this reason we have different branches in the holy Church, as for example when Saint Paul spoke about the gifts of the Holy Spirit in chapter 12 of the First Epistle to the Corinthians. He said there are different gifts but the Spirit is one. In the Church there are Apostles, there are teachers, there are priests, there are prophets, there are ordinary persons. All these may be different in rank, but all of them are holy.

You say "may all be partakers of God's truth". Partakers of God's truth inside holiness and not outside holiness. Our Lord God said that the good earth may give thirty, sixty and one hundred. These are degrees, but all of them are fruitful and good, although they vary. But as for the plants which were surrounded by thorns and withered away, we cannot say they were good, nor was the land from which the seeds were taken by sparrows.

Question 7

If a homosexual goes to the church and repents and abstains from homosexual activity, how is he viewed in the eyes of God if desires about men remain?

I want to say that sometimes repentance may take steps. The first step of repentance is to abstain from the action of sin. Sometimes the person abstains from the action of sin and at the same time still has the desire. He is now clean in flesh but not clean in spirit.

The second step is to change his mind and change his desires. In the Epistle to the Romans, chapter 12, the Apostle says: *"I beseech you therefore, brethren, by the mercies of God, that you present your bodies a living sacrifice, holy, acceptable to God, which is your reasonable service. And do not be conformed to this world, but be transformed by the renewing of your mind"* (Rom. 12: 1). A person may have another concept, another idea, another way of thinking about the world. He does not look at sin as pleasure but as defilement. He may change his mind, and in changing his mind he may change his desires also. It may take steps.

The first step of repentance is to leave sin, not to do it. But the perfection of repentance is to hate sin, and sin will not be suitable for the person's new nature in our Lord Jesus Christ.

Our great teacher Saint John the Apostle said that the son of God cannot sin: cannot, because he is the son of God. His nature has changed. This is the renewal of life. **As pastors, our work is to guide people toward the renewal of their life,** to stress on a new point, to give them practice in spiritual life. Day by day they find spiritual life not only acceptable but also favourable and **they find their pleasure in God, their pleasure in spiritual life.**

Question 8

Does the Coptic Church have a view on the use of artificial contraception?

Yes, we accept it if it is not a way of abortion. This means if it is used to avoid, rather than terminate, a pregnancy. However, once a pregnancy has occurred, than it is a sin to abort the baby, even if its age is only one hour. So, it is acceptable only to prevent pregnancy.

THE ORDINATION OF WOMEN

The first point on which I want to speak to you is our respect to the Holy Bible. Of course, everyone may say that they respect the Holy Bible, but in practice this is not always the case.

Our Respect to the Holy Bible

Many people depend on their minds more than they depend on the verses of the Bible. They depend on their intelligence, on their own understanding, not on the Bible. We are ready to have the Bible as the basis of our dogma, the basis of our theology, and see what the Bible says. If we read for example the Book of Proverbs, chapter 3, verse 5, it is written: *"Trust in the Lord with all your heart, and lean not on your understanding."* (Pro 3:5).

People may differ in their understanding, therefore, we may find many dogmas and many different concepts of theology. This warning is repeated in chapter 14, verse 12: *"There is a way that seems right to a man but its end is the way of death"* (Pro 14:12) and the same verse is found in chapter 16, verse 25: *"There is a way that seems right to a man but its end is the way of death."* (Pro. 16:25).

A person may think that his mind is sound, that his understanding of theology is suitable for him, but this may at a certain times, be in contradiction with Biblical teachings. **We should respect the Bible more than our minds.** This was the commandment of God since the beginning.

For example, if we read what our Lord God said to Joshua, the disciple of Moses, who came after him, we find Him saying: *"This Book of the Law shall not depart from your mouth, but you shall meditate in it day and night, that you may observe to do according to all that is written in it. For then you will make your way prosperous, and then you will have good success"* (Josh. 1: 8).

And it is mentioned many times that Moses did according to what the Lord had commanded him. And in the Sermon on the Mount, in Saint Matthew's Gospel, chapter 5, verse 17, our Lord Jesus Christ commanded us not to add and not to omit, and gave a punishment for this. And as I said in my first lecture, quoting from the Epistle to the Galatians, chapter 1, verses 8 and 9, the holy Apostle says: *"But even if we (the Apostles), or an angel from heaven, preach any other Gospel to you than what we have preached to you, let him be accursed"* (Gal. 1:8-9) (and in other translations, "let him be anathematised").

We have to respect the Bible and its teaching. I say this because once I heard some scholars saying: "Oh, the first eleven chapters of the Book of Genesis are mythology. The story of Jonah the Prophet is mythology. Some of the prophecies of Ezekiel are mythology". **People began to subject the Holy Bible to their minds instead of subjecting their minds to the Holy Bible.** What they accept will be alright. If not, they will

34

not respect what they do not accept in the Holy Bible. So their respect to the Holy Bible is not as it should be.

Some people may say: "Oh, this is written in the Old Testament. We do not accept it. We accept only what is written in the New Testament". **How can we refuse the words of God in the Old Testament?**

Once I was discussing some points with one of the hierarchies of the church, and I quoted verses from Saint Paul, he said to me: "Oh, this is what was said by Saint Paul and not by our Lord Jesus Christ". Then I asked him: "Are the words of Saint Paul inspired or not?" He thought and said: "Yes, they are inspired". Then I said: "Then these are the words of God inspired by the Holy Spirit".

Let us read two verses which may be useful to us. In the Second Epistle to Timothy, chapter 3, verses 15 and 16, it is written: *"...and that from childhood you have known the Holy Scriptures, which are able to make you wise for salvation through faith which is in Christ Jesus. All Scripture is given by inspiration of God, and is profitable for doctrine, for reproof, for correction, for instruction in righteousness."* (2Ti 3:15-16) And also Saint Peter said that these Books of the Scriptures are spoken by holy men led by the Holy Spirit.

Dogmas and theology need a spirit of humility. The humble person does not put himself higher than the Holy Scripture. To accept or not to accept, to omit or not to omit, is not humility. As I said earlier, some people, when they notice that the Holy Scriptures are against homosexuals, they attack the Holy Scriptures in order to defend homosexuality. If they see that the Holy Scriptures do not allow ordination of women, they are ready to attack the teachings of the Bible in order to please women.

Now I would like to deal with the subject of the ordination of women. First, as an introduction, I want to say that **women are our mothers, our sisters, and to us, our spiritual daughters. We respect them, we love them, we pray for them,** and we give them responsibilities in the Church.

Women In The Coptic Church

In the Coptic Church we have thousands of women as Sunday School teachers. In Cairo alone we have between ten to fifteen thousand females as Sunday School teachers. In our Seminary and Coptic Institute we have four ladies teaching in the Seminary: one teaches the Old Testament, another the Hebrew Language, and two teach the history of the Church. In every church we have women organising and supervising social activities. We also have women in many of the councils of churches. They have many responsibilities.

Women In The Holy Bible

The responsibilities of women were given to them from the beginning. We can mention many prophetesses. Miriam the sister of Moses was a prophetess. Deborah the Judge of Israel was a prophetess, Huldah was a prophetess. Anna, at the time of the birth of our Lord, was a prophetess. They may be prophetesses, no problem. They may be queens, such as Esther who was a queen and she was a saviour for a whole nation. This is all right, a wise woman who could save her nation. We know that Mary Magdalene was delegated by our Lord Jesus Christ to announce the happy news of the Resurrection to the eleven Apostles.

Many women gave their houses to be churches in the Apostolic Age. Among them was Saint Mary the mother of Saint Mark the Evangelist. Her house became a church. This is mentioned in the Book of Acts (Acts 12: 12). Also the house of Aquila and Priscilla and Lydia as is mentioned in chapter 16 of the Epistle to the Romans.

Many women ministered to the Lord. They served Him, and some of these women were mentioned in the eighth chapter of Saint Luke's Gospel: *"Now it came to pass, afterward, that He went through every city and village, preaching and bringing the glad tidings of the kingdom of God. And the twelve were with Him, and certain women who had been healed of evil spirits and infirmities - Mary called Magdalene, out of whom had come seven demons, and Joanna the wife of Chuza, Herod's steward, and Susanna, and many others who provided for Him from their substance"* (Luke. 8: 1-3).

They were servants of God. Beside the Cross of our Lord, women were the majority, there was only one man, Saint John the Evangelist, and the rest were women.

Priesthood In The Holy Bible

Women may be full of love and emotion, and if they devote their love and emotion to Christ they can be very helpful. **But in spite of this we cannot find in the whole Bible one single example of a woman being a priest.** Perhaps God called women for other responsibilities. Priesthood is a Divine call and it is quite obvious in the Holy Bible that women were called for many, many responsibilities, but not for priesthood.

The first priesthood was the priesthood of the great patriarchs of the church: Father Abraham, Father Noah, Father Isaac, Father Jacob. All these were men. The second kind of priesthood was the priesthood of Melchizedek, who was mentioned in Genesis, chapter 14, and in Hebrews chapter 7, and the priesthood of Aaron and his sons. All of them were men. **There was not a single woman priest in all of the Old Testament.** If God had wanted it, all right. Who can prevent God?

The firstborn children who were sanctified to God before choosing the priesthood of Moses, Aaron and the sons of Aaron- were all men. When the Lord Jesus Christ chose the twelve Apostles to be the first priests or archpriests, or the first bishops or ecumenical bishops, they were all men. And the first bishops consecrated by them were also men.

Priesthood in Church Tradition

Throughout history there is not one example of a female priest. Not one example in Bible, nor in Tradition, and we have to trace and follow the teaching of the Bible, because the Christian life is a life handed down from one generation to another generation. For example, in the first Epistle to the Corinthians chapter 11, when Saint Paul spoke about the Eucharist, he said: *"For I received from the Lord that which I also delivered to you"* (1Cor. 11: 23).

God delivered dogmas, theology and rites to the Apostles, and the Apostles delivered them to their disciples, to the first bishops, and they delivered them to another generation, until these dogmas reached our day. For this reason, Saint Paul said to his disciple Timothy, who was the Bishop of Ephesus, *"And the things that you have heard from me among many witnesses, commit these to faithful men who will be able to teach others also"* (2Tim. 2: 2). Teaching was handed down from Saint Paul to Timothy, and from Timothy to faithful men, and from these faithful men to others.

This is the Tradition, the Apostolic Tradition, which we received from the age of the Apostles, throughout all ages, till now. **And, of course, if God had wanted to call women for priesthood, He would have done so, in the same way as He called women to be prophetesses.**

The Church is a collection of the members of our Lord Jesus Christ. Every member performs a certain duty. We cannot say that all members are the same. Every member in the

39

Body of our Lord has its dignity, its respect, its work, its importance. We cannot say that all members may be heads, all may be eyes, may be arms, may be hearts! We cannot say this. **If a woman is not called to be the head, perhaps she is called to be the heart, and no difference.**

Every member has its own work in the Church, and this also is what was said by the Apostle when he was speaking about the gifts of the Holy Spirit. We may read the First Epistle to the Corinthians, chapter 12: *"But now indeed there are many members, yet one body. And God has appointed these in the church: first apostles, second prophets, third teachers, after that miracles, then gifts of hearings, helps, administrations, varieties of tongues. Are all apostles? Are all prophets? Are all teachers? Are all workers of miracles? Do all have gifts of hearings?"* (1Cor. 12: 20, 28-30). But God gave every member its own work.

Men and women cannot be rivals in a certain responsibility. Women can perform many duties which are useful in the church, but they were not called for priesthood. We are not to be blamed for this because this is not our teaching, it is the Biblical teaching. If you can find one single example in the Bible, whether in the Old Testament or in the New Testament, we are ready to accept it. We are not against the words of God. **We accept the words of God. But we cannot add new teachings.**

Who Is The Head?

Then, who does the New Testament say is the head, man or woman? This is mentioned in Ephesus, chapter 5, and many times in the First Epistle to the Corinthians. *"I want you to know that the head of every man is Christ, the head of woman is man. For man is not from woman, but woman from man. Nor was man created for the woman, but woman for the man. For this reason the woman ought to have a symbol of authority on her head, because of the angels"* (1Cor. 11: 3, 8-10).

Man and woman co-operate together, but man is the head of woman. If woman is headed by man in the house, can she be the head of all the congregation in the church, among whom is her husband who is her head? Or may she say to him: 'You are my head in the house, but I am your head in the church?' I do not know how to find a solution for this problem.

Also, the priest represents our Lord Jesus Christ.

The Virgin Mary And Priesthood

If women were called to priesthood, the first woman in the world would have been the Virgin Mary. **No woman in the world is more holy than Saint Mary.** And no woman in the whole world is more worthy- if it is a matter of worthiness- than the Virgin Mary. And Saint Mary the Virgin did not claim to be a priest. She was the spiritual mother of all the Apostles, but she did not claim to be a priest.

Deaconesses and Serving the Altar

Not only is this concerning priesthood, but also the work of deacons in serving the altar. When the Apostles consecrated the seven first deacons, what did they say? They said: *"Therefore, brethren, seek out from among you seven men of good reputation, full of the Holy Spirit and wisdom, whom we may appoint over this business"* (Acts 6: 3). In the history of the Church, we may find some Deaconesses, not for the service of the altar, but for social service or educational service or for discipline or for helping the priest in matters concerning women in the holy Sacraments, but not for serving the altar, not for the Holy Eucharist, not to baptise, nothing of the sort.

In the First Epistle to Timothy, chapter 2, verses 11-15, **Saint Paul does not permit women to teach men in the church.** In the Coptic Church we let women teach children or other women or girls in Sunday School, but they do not teach men.

I am sorry, I do not want women to be displeased, but this is the Holy Bible. It is not a problem: it is how to give certain gifts to certain people. **It is not being against women, but it is a matter of classifying the gifts of God.**

Now I return to Romans, chapter 12, regarding this matter, to read and see what the Holy Bible says to us: *"For I say, through the grace given to me, to everyone who is among you, not to think of himself more highly than he ought to think, but to think soberly, as God has dealt to each one a measure of faith. For as we have many members in one body, but all the members do not have the same function, so we, being many, are one body in Christ, and individually members of one another. Having then gifts differing according to the grace that is given to us, let us use them: if prophecy, let us prophesy in the proportion to our faith; or ministry..."* (Rom. 12: 3-6), and then it goes on to describe every kind of ministry. Of course women have ministries in the church, not priesthood, but many other kinds of work and responsibilities.

In the First Epistle to Timothy, the Apostle says: *"Let a woman learn in silence with all submission. And I do not permit a woman to teach or have authority over a man, but to be in silence"* (1Tim 2: 11,12). That means that the work of prayer in the Liturgy is the work of the priest. She may attend silently and not teach men or have authority over men.

Women And The Priest's Work

There are many things in the work of the priest which may not be suitable for women, for example, baptising men. How can a woman baptise men? It is not easy. If she is a bishop and ordains priests, that means that these priests will be subordinate to her, under her authority, under her hierarchy or jurisdiction. **This is contradictory to the teaching of the Holy Bible.** The Holy Anointment, how can she anoint men? How about the periods in which a woman cannot enter the church, or it is not easy for her to work, if she is a priest and pregnant in the ninth month or eighth month, or when she gives birth and must stay at home. I do not want to enter into such detail, but many other points concerning women may not help her work constantly in the church.

Church Sacraments Delivered To Men

When our Lord Jesus Christ delivered the Sacraments of the Church, He did not deliver these Sacraments to women.

For example, when He delivered Priesthood, as is mentioned in Saint John's Gospel, chapter 20, verses 21 to 23, He gave this authority to the eleven Apostles: *"Then Jesus said to them (to the eleven Apostles) again, 'Peace to you! As the Father has sent Me, I also send you.' And when He had said this, He breathed on them, and said to them, 'Receive the Holy Spirit. If you forgive the sins of any, they are forgiven them; if you retain the sins of any, they are retained.'"* (John 20:21-23) He gave this to the Apostles, to the Eleven, not to any women.

When He gave them the Sacrament of Baptism, if we read for example Saint Matthew's Gospel, chapter 28, verse 16: *"Then the eleven disciples went away into Galilee, to the mountain which Jesus had appointed for them. And when they saw Him, they worshipped Him; but some doubted. Then Jesus came and spoke to them, saying, 'All authority has been given to Me in heaven and on earth. Go therefore and make disciples of all the nations, baptising them in the name of the Father and of the Son and of the Holy Spirit, teaching them to observe all things that I have commanded you; and lo, I am with you always, even to the end of the age'"* (Matt. 28: 16-20). **He gave the authority of baptising and teaching to the Eleven.** He did not call all the women- although many women were very holy and were serving Him, as mentioned in Luke chapter 8, and those who followed Him to the Cross. But He said this to the Eleven.

And also of the Eucharist, Saint Paul said: *"For I received from the Lord that which I also delivered to you"* (1Cor. 11: 23). He received this Sacrament from the Lord. This Sacrament was also given by the Lord to the Eleven after the departure of Judas. He said to them, ***"Do this in remembrance of Me."*** He said to them: *"... teaching them to observe all things that I have commanded you"*, meaning what they were taught by our Lord Jesus Christ, and this also was for the Eleven. And He appeared to them for forty days and spoke to them about the mysteries of the kingdom of God, about all things concerning the kingdom of God, this also was to the eleven Apostles.

I think it is better for a woman to remain a woman, to work in services, and handle responsibilities which are more suitable for a woman. A bird may sing a sweet song on a tree and a lion may roar in the forest. If the bird tries to be a lion, it is not suitable. It is more beautiful for the bird, for the sparrow or the pigeon, to sing a sweet song and than to roar like a lion. And if the lion tries to sing like the bird it will not be acceptable. **Let women be in the service of women, and man in the service of man**.

Responsibilities of Women

A woman has great responsibilities. Among these responsibilities, I may mention, is having **pastoral care for children in order to prepare a new generation for the Church.** One of our problems is that women have no time to care for their children.

I can mention a holy woman in history and that is Jochebed the mother of Moses. Due to the teaching given by this holy woman to her son Moses -Moses lived in the palace of Pharaoh when he was three, four or five years old and lived the rest of the 40 years among many pharaonic worships and many idols-Moses became not only a man of faith but a hero of faith. How? **Because of the teaching of his holy mother who instilled faith in him during his childhood.**

If women take care of their children they prepare for us the priests of the Church. The priests of the Church of course were once children, and if children are well prepared, well taught and well instructed in religious teachings, by their mothers, then women will **have prepared priests without being themselves priests.**

The following are some of the questions asked by members of the congregation and the answers given by His Holiness:

Question 1

In the Church, what is the status of a bishop who ordains women? Is he still a true bishop?

In our Church no bishops ordain women. I think in all the Orthodox Churches no bishops ordain women, and I think also in the Catholic Church no bishops ordain women. I am only speaking about what we are taught from the Bible.

I also wish to say that ordaining women caused a kind of division and separation here in the Church. What benefit could the Church take from ordaining women; only conflict among the priests and bishops. Many dioceses refused to ordain women or to accept women ordained by other bishops.

There is another point I wish to mention very frankly and very openly. I am sorry to say these words, but please excuse me. The Church may try to please women by ordaining them as priests, and this is what happened here. After this, being a priest was no longer sufficient for women, they wanted to be bishops. After being ordained as bishops, it was still insufficient. Then, women began to ask the question: Is God a Man or a Woman? Of course gender is not found in Divinity. But they began to say: "Why do we say: 'Our Father who art in heaven?' Why do we not say 'Our Mother?'" And this was a problem in many meetings of the World Council of Churches, and some tried to compromise and say 'Our Parent who art in heaven'. If we try to trace all the verses in which God is mentioned as Father in the Bible, we'll find so many! This suggestion means that we have to change the Bible!

If we change the Bible, what will be said of us by other religions? They will say that this Book is not the Book of God; you are trying to make alterations, and these are not the words inspired by the Holy Spirit in the Holy Bible!

Question 2

What advice would you give to an Anglican priest should the General Synod agree to ordain women to priesthood?

I wish and pray that this may not happen. That is what I can say. We are friends of the Anglican Church and we do not want to have any division or separation in the Church for the sake of the good of the Church. We pray that this may not happen.

Question 3

Nowadays many people question the exact inspiration of certain parts of the Bible. What do you say against this?

I want to say openly that criticisms of Biblical teachings have had many defects. Let me give you an example, and I say this because we live in non-Christian countries and know the impression which takes place:a professor in a theological college may teach the Gospels, he begins to teach the Gospel of Saint John, and in his study he may say: "Oh, who was the author of Saint John's Gospel? Was he one of the disciples of the Lord Jesus Christ or another John who lived in the second century?" and finally he may conclude that it was another John.

Then it may be said to us: "You do not know your Bible: whether it was written by God, by the Holy Spirit, by Jesus Christ, by the disciples or by other people in the second century..." These points of criticism may be used against Christianity and published on a large scale. You know for example, that Dedacht, who had a great discussion in America with a Christian priest, took nearly all his points from this style of biblical criticism. Many points are taken to attack Christianity. If you say that some parts of the Bible are mythology, non-Christians may take this point and say: 'Here is a witness from the Christians, from the leaders of Christianity, from the priests, that this is mythology.'

My brothers, take great care when you publish such books and put in your mind the effect, the impression and the reaction to such things. Now they question the inspiration of some Books of the Bible. This means that the matter is doubtful, because it is a matter of argument whether it is inspired or not. This means that the Tradition which we received from the Apostles is under discussion: I mean the Tradition concerning the Holy Books of the Bible which we received from the Ecumenical Councils is also under discussion; not yet accepted. Is this good for the faith of the common people? If it is accepted to a certain extent for seminaries or students of theology, can this be accepted by all common people to look at their Holy Bible as a doubtful Book? What is the benefit?

Once a student said: "I was full of faith, and for this reason I went to a seminary to be a scholar, and after some years I lost my faith, because everything which I accepted in a spiritual way began to be taken as a questionable matter, a matter of criticism, whether to accept or not". And what happened? Christianity began to be a kind of philosophy, not a simple religion as Saint Paul said.

I want to read you some verses from Saint Paul's First Epistle to the Corinthians. Although he was a great scholar at his time and studied at the feet of Gamaliel the great professor of his generation, what did Saint Paul say? He said: "And my speech and my preaching were not with persuasive words of human wisdom, but in demonstration of the Spirit and of power, that your faith should not be in the wisdom of men but in the power of God. However, we speak wisdom among those who are mature, yet not the wisdom of this age, nor of the rulers of this age, who are coming to nothing" (1Cor. 2: 4-6). And he also says, in the same chapter: *"These things we also speak, not in words which man's wisdom teaches but which the Holy Spirit teaches, comparing spiritual things with spiritual"* (1Cor. 2: 13).

Saint Paul was the most educated Apostle at his time. **But he did not use the wisdom of the world. He used simplicity. He used the words of the Holy Spirit.** But now we are trying to use the wisdom of the world or the wisdom of men. What about the respect of the Bible? We try to criticise the Bible. **We try to subject the Bible to our minds, not to surrender to the inspiration of the Holy Spirit.**

Once a person pointed at his head and said: "That was the fruit from which Adam was forbidden to eat. It was the tree of knowledge". Adam knew many things which were profitable to him, but he wanted also to eat from the tree of knowledge of good and evil. He knew only the knowledge of good, then he began to know the knowledge of evil; to suspect everything, to doubt everything. It is as if theology is philosophy, and not good philosophy, but philosophy of doubts! In our seminaries, should we give our people the spirit of the Bible, or stress on criticism of the Bible?

Question 4

In the Holy Eucharist, the priest takes the Holy Body and Blood of Jesus in his hands. The Blessed Virgin Mary took Jesus in her hands. Why should another woman not be allowed to take the Body and Blood of Jesus?

Women are allowed to take the Body and Blood of Jesus in their mouths, not only in their hands- inside them. And when we say that the Virgin Mary was holding Jesus in her hand, **this was not a kind of Eucharist. This was motherhood. There is great difference between motherhood and priesthood.** This is one thing and that is something else. A holy woman may have our Lord Jesus Christ appearing to her, but this is not the Eucharist. We should put an exact definition for everything.

When the Virgin Mary was holding our Lord Jesus Christ in her hands, was she performing or officiating a matter of Priesthood or Eucharist? As for the Body and Blood of our Lord Jesus Christ, all the congregation takes of the Body and Blood. There is no discrimination between women and men. All of them partake in the Holy Communion; no difference. The Eucharist is how to pray that this Prosphora, this holy bread, may be transubstantiated into the Body of Jesus Christ, and the wine into His Blood. But this was not happening with our Lady Saint Mary- it was something else.

Question 5

How would you explain Saint Paul's words about woman for man and not man for woman?

51

He is speaking about the story of creation, because man was created first and then woman was created afterwards to help him, to be a good helper equivalent to him, because man and woman before God are equals. Man is not preferred nor woman but the deeds of every person may put him first or last. Before God, in their deeds, they are equal. But in their properties, in their responsibilities, they are different. Men do not ask: Why do we not give birth to children? Everyone is in his own position.

Question 6

Is there not a sense in which all Christians are priests? How does this sort of priesthood differ from ordaining priesthood?

We are all priests in the spiritual meaning, as David the Prophet said: *"...the lifting up of my hands as the evening sacrifice"* (Ps. 14: 1). And it was said: *"the sacrifice of thanksgiving, the sacrifice of spiritual singing."* This is a kind of spiritual priesthood, not the priesthood of the Holy Mysteries. *"Let my prayer be set before You as incense"* (Ps. 141: 2), is this priesthood? This may be said by a woman or a man. This is the spiritual meaning, not the literal meaning of priesthood, which is serving the altar and officiating the Holy Mysteries of the Church.

Question 7

Why do some Churches refuse to give the Holy Eucharist to Christian children under 13 years until they are confirmed?

In our Church we give Holy Communion to any child, and we also give the holy Chrism to the child from the beginning of his life, just after Baptism. I think this is only known in the Catholic Church. We give the Body and Blood of our Lord to the child from the very beginning of his life, after Baptism.

Thank you for listening, and I am happy to be among you. I am in need for your prayers, all of you, to return to my country safely and carry on my responsibilities.

My best wishes to the Anglican Church, its bishops and its priests, wishing for this Church all prosperity.

www.ingramcontent.com/pod-product-compliance
Lightning Source LLC
Chambersburg PA
CBHW060622030426
42337CB00018B/3141